Unit 10

Think Outside the Box

Contents

Tube Race

Get set! Go! Race!
Luke did not win the game.
It did not go quick. It sat
in the tube.

Do not fume, Luke.
June got a big cube.
The cube can fix it.
Yes. The big tube is up.

Who can win it?
Get set! Go! Race!
Luke and June did not
win. It did not go quick.

Do not fume, Luke.
Mike will not use the
same size. It will fit in
the tube!

Who can win it?
Get set! Go! Race!
Luke and June win it!
Good fix, Mike.

The Sad Duke

Duke Ike sat.

The duke was quite sad.

The mule was sick.

Who can help?

Wade can hum a tune.
Duke Ike did not like it.
Kate gave him a cute cat.
Duke Ike did not like it.

Jan can hop on a cube.
Dale can make a joke.
Duke Ike did not like it.
Duke Ike was quite sad.

The cat ran quick. It made
Jan quake. Jan dove on
Dale. Dale bit a lip.
Duke Ike was mad!

Dale did not get the cat.
But Dale got Wade!
The duke was not sad.
Good job, cat!

Pete and Eve

This is Pete and Eve.
Pete said, "Does Eve ride
with me?
Yes, she does!"

They like to play a game.
Eve can hide.
Pete, come get Eve!
Eve is good at the game.

Pete and Eve like Zeke.
Zeke can nap with Pete.
Does Zeke nap with Eve?
No. He can tug with Eve.

Eve and Pete joke a lot.
Eve gave Zeke a hat.
Pete can get a red cape.
Eve can get a wig.

17

Pete and Eve bake.
Pete can make a hot
cake. Yum! Eve can make
a big mess. Yuck!

Jamie Grill/Getty Images

Pete Can Fix It

"Pete, come here," said Mom.
"Does it look fine?"
"No," said Pete.
"Yuck! I can fix it."

Pete got a tan cube.
He got a red jet. Pete set
it in.
He set in a bus and van.

Pete got a big red bin.
He set in Fox, Cat, and Pig.
"Zeke gave Pig to me,"
said Pete.

Pete got a wide box.
He set in a cape and
fake nose.
"I can be Dad," said Pete.
He set in a big hat and wig.

Eve and Zeke came.
"Can we play Pete?"
"Yes, Pete. You did fix it,"
said Mom.

See It?

Take the map.
Come on, let us go!
Let us see.
Let us meet.

Can you see a big bus?
Let us get on the bus.
We need the bus to go.
I can see a lot. Beep!

Tom can dig a big hole.
Tom can set in a seed.
Can you see a bee? Eek!

Can you see the reef?
It is deep. Dee can use a
big reel.
Does Dee have it? Yes!

Let us go see a queen.
Can you see a
queen wave?
Quick! Let us get in line.
Yes! You can meet a queen.

Deb Bee

Queen Zee is in the hive.
Deb Bee is a teen bee.
Deb can feed Queen Zee.
But Deb is sad.

Deb does not like the hive.
"Come to my hive in a
week," said June Bee.
"Yes, I can!" said Deb.

Deb Bee can seek the hive.
Deb can see it and Deb can
see June Bee.
Queen Jo can meet Deb.

Queen Jo does not like Deb.
"Peel it! Cut it! Fix it!"
"I need to go home,"
said Deb.

Deb can see the hive.
Deb can go in deep.
Deb can see Queen Zee.
Deb Bee can hug six feet!

We Can Save!

Dave can make it.
Dave can use a tube.
Dave can use a cube, too.
It is so cute, Dave!

Did Pete come to play?
No. Pete has a seed.
He can set it in deep.
It can get big in the sun.

Lee has a good rule.
Lee does not keep it on.
Lee can save a lot.
Can you name a rule?

Nile can see a big bin.
He can get to it.
He can set it in. Where
can you see a big bin?

Image Source/Getty Images

Who can save? We can!
Can you help? I hope so.
We need to be wise.
We can save a lot!

42

Tube Race WORD COUNT: 94

DECODABLE WORDS
Target Phonics Elements
Long *u, u_e:* cube, fume, June, Luke, tube, use

HIGH-FREQUENCY WORDS
good, who
Review: a, and, do, the

The Sad Duke
WORD COUNT: 101

DECODABLE WORDS
Target Phonics Elements
Long *u, u_e:* cube, cute, duke, mule, tune

HIGH-FREQUENCY WORDS
good, who
Review: a, help, the, was

Pete and Eve WORD COUNT: 98

DECODABLE WORDS
Target Phonics Elements
Long *e: e_e, e; e_e:* Eve, Pete, Zeke; *e:* he, we

HIGH-FREQUENCY WORDS
come, does
Review: a, and, are, good, is, look, play, the, they, to, with

---

Pete Can Fix It
WORD COUNT: 105

DECODABLE WORDS
Target Phonics Elements
Long *e: e_e, e; e_e:* Eve, Pete, Zeke; *e:* he, me, we

HIGH-FREQUENCY WORDS
come, does
Review: a, and, here, I, look, play, said, you

See It?
WORD COUNT: 101

DECODABLE WORDS
Target Phonics Elements
Long *e, ee:* bee, beep, Dee, deep, eek, meet, need, queen, reef, reel, see, seed

HIGH-FREQUENCY WORDS
come, does
Review: a, have, I, is, the, to, we, you

43

Deb Bee

DECODABLE WORDS

Target Phonics Elements

Long *e, ee:* bee, deep, feed, feet, meet, peel, queen, see, seek, teen, week, Zee

HIGH-FREQUENCY WORDS

come, does

Review: a, I, is, my, said, the, to

Week 3 | **We Can Save**

DECODABLE WORDS

Target Phonics Elements

Review Long *a, a_e;* Long *i, i_e;* Long *o, o_e;* Long *u, u_e;* Long *e:* *e_e, e, ee;* *a_e:* make, save; ***i_e:*** Nile, wise; ***o, o_e:*** no, so, hope; ***u_e:*** cube, cute, rule, tube, use; ***e_e:*** Pete; ***e:*** be, he, we; ***ee:*** deep, keep, Lee, need, see, seed

HIGH-FREQUENCY WORDS

come, has, look, play, too, where, who

Review: a, is, the, to, you

HIGH-FREQUENCY WORDS TAUGHT TO DATE

Grade K

a
and
are
can
come
do
does
for
go
good
has
have
he
help
here
I
is
like
little
look
me
my
of
play
said
see
she
the
they
this
to
too
want
was
we
what
where
who
with
you

DECODING SKILLS TAUGHT TO DATE

Initial and final consonant *m*; short *a*; initial *s*; initial and final consonant *p*; initial and final consonant *t*; initial and medial vowel *i*; initial and final consonant *n*; initial *c*; initial and medial vowel *o*; initial and final *d*; initial consonant *h*; initial and medial vowel *e*; initial consonants *f* and *r*; initial and final consonant *b*; initial consonant *l*; initial consonant *k*; final digraph *ck*; initial and medial vowel *u*; initial and final *g*; initial *w*; final consonant *x*; initial consonant *v*; initial consonant *j*; initial consonant *qu*; initial consonant *z*; initial consonant *y*; long *a, a_e*; long *i, i_e*; long *o, o_e*; long *u, u_e*; long *e, ee, e_e*